JOY

JOY

Louis Evely

TRANSLATED BY BRIAN
AND MARIE-CLAUDE THOMPSON

HERDER AND HERDER

1968
HERDER AND HERDER NEW YORK
232 Madison Avenue, New York 10016

Original edition: *Le chemin de joie,*
published by the author.

Nihil obstat: Brendan W. Lawlor, Censor Librorum
Imprimatur: ✠ Robert F. Joyce, Bishop of Burlington
November 21, 1967

CONTENTS

INTRODUCTION
JOY   7

THE FIRST STATION
MARY MAGDALENE   19

THE SECOND STATION
THE DISCIPLES OF EMMAUS   29

THE THIRD STATION
PETER   53

THE FOURTH STATION
THOMAS   61

THE FIFTH STATION
PAUL   77

THE SIXTH STATION
MARY   87

THE SEVENTH STATION
THE ASCENSION   93

INTRODUCTION

JOY

I AM going to talk about the joy of God—the joy he left us.

Jesus told us: "Peace I leave with you; my peace I give to you; not as the world gives do I give to you" (Jn. 14, 27).

But he told us also: "These things I have spoken to you, that my joy may be in you, and that your joy may be full" (Jn. 15, 11).

"Your sorrow will turn into joy" (Jn. 16, 20).

When you have become penetrated with the joy of God, all of your sorrows will turn into joy, all of your trials will be graces; you will recognize your faults, you will be sorry for them, and they will be forgiven so that they may become happy faults. They will remind you only of the goodness, the tenderness, the joy with which God forgives them.

When you become penetrated with the joy of God, God will become God again, he will become a Father again, and we will again become his children.

The Christian religion is a religion of joy. The Gospel is the good news, and in spite of our occasionally melancholy appearance, we are messengers of joy, witnesses of the resurrection.

Joy is a command from Christ: "If you loved me, you would have rejoiced . . ." (Jn. 14, 28).

"I will not leave you desolate; I will come to you" (Jn. 14, 18).

"I will see you again and your hearts will rejoice, and no

one will take your joy from you . . . ask, and you will receive, that your joy may be full" (Jn. 16, 22–24).

Christian joy differentiates us from the world and is the means of our apostolate: "Truly, truly, I say to you, you will weep and lament, but the world will rejoice; you will be sorrowful, but your sorrow will turn into joy" (Jn. 16, 20). For Christ sent us the Comforter "whom the world cannot receive, because it neither sees him nor knows him; you know him, for he dwells with you, and will be in you" (Jn. 14, 17).

Indeed, Christ made us the depositaries of his joy.

What have we done with his joy?

Strangely enough, we do not cherish the joy of God. We are much more inclined to mourn with Christ than to rejoice with him.

We can understand Lent, we can take part in it. During this forty-day period we devote ourselves to penance, compassion, and mortification.

But how lax we are during the days which follow our sorrow! We do not even know how to rejoice! We devote ourselves to doing absolutely nothing. The day is coming when the Spirit of Truth will breathe upon us, and we do not joyfully await it.

At Calvary, there were still a few of the faithful who remained, some women and one man. They were the poor representatives of our species. But at the time of the resurrection, no one was there, no one believed any longer, everyone had despaired. Jesus had to convert all of them one by one to the reality of his joy.

You have often followed the way of the cross. This is a good way; it is beneficial, advisable, and necessary.

But have you ever followed the way of joy?

It does not exist in our devotions, and yet the Church invites us after Easter to "stations of joy" which should be as much frequented and meditated upon as are the stations of the way of the cross.

We are going to do that together now. We are going to make a pilgrimage on the way of joy, we are going to pause a long while at each station of joy, we are going to meditate upon each account of the apparitions of the risen Christ, we are going to repeat with him all of those experiences by means of which—with great tenderness, patience, and affection—he tried to awaken his apostles to his joy, to convince them of his resurrection, to transform their sorrows into joy.

It is necessary for us to follow this way!

All too often, after Easter, we go on vacation in our religious life. We have worked hard during Lent. We reason: Christ is risen . . . He is happy . . . He is safely in heaven. We can do no more for him. Now that his hour of suffering is over, his way and ours can part. *We* are going to go on with our life and suffering here below. *He* is in beatitude.

Is there not something hard and selfish in mourning with a friend so long as he is in distress, and refusing to rejoice with him when his trial has ended? For the greatest testimony to our friendship, the greatest pleasure of friendship, is to share the joy of a friend.

We act as though we are specialists in bad news, when in fact we have been told by Christ that we are to be the bearers of glad rejoicing.

Why are we selfish when we do not rejoice with a friend? Because to share in the happiness of another presupposes a disinterestedness on our part, a delicacy of the heart, a detachment from our self.

After Lent has ended, we have yet to make the greatest mortification, the greatest renouncement: we have to make for God the sacrifice of being happy! This will prove the sincerity of our friendship. We have to give God the joy of seeing us happy because of him, to tell him: "You did so much for us, you loved us so much and suffered so much for us, that we now want to give you the reward of seeing us happy. We want to be happy with faith, happy with confidence, happy to be with you." We should depend so much on God, be so united and bound to him, that when we look into ourselves we find ourselves alive with his joy.

The true love, the true faith, the true disinterestedness which Lent leads us towards, should lead us also to true happiness.

* * *

To be sure, Christian joy is not an easy contentment, a naïve self-satisfaction, or even a naïve satisfaction for the sake of others. It is a *sadness overcome.*

12

Christian joy bursts out in the beatitudes: Blessed are the poor, for theirs is the kingdom of heaven! Blessed are those who mourn! Blessed are those who hunger and thirst for righteousness! Blessed are those who are persecuted!

But we must be careful: when the beatitudes are proclaimed in a Christian assembly, very often we reach the conclusion: "Well, now I have to become poor, I have to hunger and thirst, and be persecuted." We miss the point: that we have to be blessed, we have to be happy! Happy poor, happy persecuted, happy afflicted, happy unhappy!

This is an impossible task, of course. But if we do not ask God to let the impossible happen, we do not ask him to reveal himself as God. If we ask of him only the possible, we ask of him what we can and should do ourselves. But God takes pleasure only in doing what surpasses us. God shows himself, manifests himself only in achieving the impossible, in showing us that he is capable of making appear in us this impossible thing: his joy in our sadness, his happiness in our poverty, his beatitude in our distress.

Truly, everything which we have closed to happiness, we have closed to God. We shut God out from all those areas in ourselves where we are resigned not to let joy, hope, confidence, and love enter.

Our sadness measures exactly our attachment to ourselves. It denounces our selfishness.

The place we give to joy is the place we give to God. We believe no more in him than in joy.

Too many Christians have a religion of the cross. They

bear witness to the absence of God. They mount guard in front of the *empty* tomb. They keep a severe, gloomy, bitter watch.

But our religion is not the religion of absence, but of presence, of the real presence of God. We are Christian only if we bear witness to our encounter with God, to the fact that he has spoken to us, that he has healed us as no one else could have done.

The apostles, once converted, never again regretted the presence of Jesus in his flesh. St. Paul says proudly: "Though we once regarded Christ from a human point of view, we regard him thus no longer" (2 Cor. 5, 16). St. Ignatius of Antioch said: "Heavenly things are much more eloquent than earthly things. Our Lord Jesus Christ manifests himself much better now that he is with the Father!" The early Christians knew Christ better, for he was present in spirit among them.

Taking our example from the primitive Church, our apostolate too is this: to have so generous a behavior, a love so alive among us, a heart so filled with joy and faith, that those who meet us can only explain it by admitting in their turn that Christ is risen from the dead.

* * *

God, when he revealed himself, did this incredible thing: he filled the world with joy!

14

There are two things Christ reproached his apostles for: fear and sadness. "Why are you afraid, O men of little faith? It is I; have no fear! Woman, why are you weeping, whom do you seek? What is this conversation which you are holding with each other as you walk, that you are sad? O foolish men, and slow of heart to believe!"

Jansenists that we are, we have invented a religion of sadness and fear. Invariably we create a God in our image. Because we do not love him very much, we are led to think that he does not love us much. Because we do not worry much about him, we imagine that he does not worry very much about us. Because we are not very happy with him, we conclude that he is not very happy with us.

But the whole of relevation protests. Revelation teaches us that God is not like us, that we should not consult how we feel towards him in order to know how he feels towards us, that God is good even if we are bad, that God loves us even if we do not love him, that God loved us first.

When God revealed himself, he tore every veil, he exceeded every limit. He dazzled, he amazed everybody. When God showed himself as God, it was a revelation of joy.

God was infinitely better than anyone imagined. God was young, tender, gracious, kind, indulgent, audacious, understanding, gay, like a child, happy. God was God!

We expected a judge, an avenger, an executioner, and it was a child who was born. We were preparing for a rendering of accounts, we were going "to put ourselves right with

God," and a baby was stretching out his arms to us, asking for our love, protection, and tenderness. All the confidence we never dared to have in God, *he* had in us!

The Gospel begins with an immense gladness. There are announcements, promises, miracles, calls, an unceasing wonder. The world is astounded, everyone receives infinitely beyond what he thought possible. Elizabeth, the sterile, gives birth. Zachary, the incredulous, prophesies. The virgin becomes a mother. The shepherds talk with the angels. The wise men give all that they have. Simeon no longer fears death.

And the multitude, at the multiplication of the bread, suddenly learned that they were not hungry. How astonished they were! Oh, the moment before, they would have fought one another for a little piece of bread. They were in a sulky mood because they were without provisions. But now each one held in his hand the miraculous bread which had come from a word out of the mouth of God, and to hold it so, marvelously satisfied the heart of each one. Slowly they were raising to their lips this sacred bread, this bread from heaven which was giving life again to the world. They were communicating, they were closing their eyes; they were pausing, they had too much, they were too rich. Their hearts were aching and they were crying. They needed nothing more, they no longer wanted to eat.

And the cripples and the lepers, when they learned that they were healed, discovered that they had not really needed a cure in order to be happy. They saw that they had a long way yet to go, that their healing was only a provisory step.

Up till then, they had thought they were suffering only from sickness, from a handicap, from a fear of the future. But they now realized that they had been tormented by something else: they had doubted God, asking themselves why he was angry with them, what they were guilty of, why he had so unjustly and indifferently and capriciously burdened them with disease and deformity.

Even the incredulous, who denied him, ignored him, cursed him, even they knew now that what they had been most in need of was to be able to believe in the goodness of God. When they perceived, in the flash of the miracle, the affection of God smiling upon them, they were immediately fulfilled, they no longer desired anything else, they found out what they were in need of—that it was *not* to be cured.

All of them, now, were willing to become ill again; they would be good patients; they would be happy in their illness, they would know that they were loved.

Our greatest mistake is to believe that we always lack only one thing, just one little thing, in order to be happy: some money, a promotion, some luck; that this illness be cured or that trial ended.

If we think thus, then we will never be happy, for there will always be another illness, another trial, some unexpected catastrophe.

It is God we lack. And the unexpected thing about God is that he does not fail us: we fail him.

We must learn to be happy immediately, we must begin to be happy right away—or we will never be happy. For the eternal life, like the joy which it engenders, always begins now.

THE FIRST STATION

MARY MAGDALENE

NOTHING is stranger, more disconcerting, more misleading than a manifestation of God. We always take God to be different from what he is.

He began by living among us, putting all the love he was capable of into his prayer, his family, his work, his friendships, and this was the stupefying summation: that after thirty years, no one (not even his precursor) had noticed him. "Among you stands one whom you do not know" (Jn. 1, 26). "I myself did not know him" (Jn. 1, 31. 33).

For the next three years he preached, explained, acted, performed miracles, prophesied, and yet his most faithful companions, the witnesses of all his works, the confidants of all his words, still did not know who he was: "Have I been with you so long, and yet you do not know me, Philip?" (Jn. 14, 9).

After his resurrection he appeared to those who loved him most, and none of them recognized him. Magdalene thought that he was the gardener. As for the disciples of Emmaus, their eyes were kept from recognizing him; and the apostles, seeing a stranger standing on the beach, did not dare to ask him "Who are you?", for they well knew that he was the Lord.

God will of necessity always be a hidden God. His loudest cry is silence. If he does not manifest himself to us, we will say that he hides himself. And if he manifests himself, we will accuse him of veiling himself. Ah! it is not easy for God to make himself known to us!

God is God only if he surprises us, disappoints us, disconcerts us. He is too large for our heart to contain. If he did what we expected of him, he would not be God, but an idea or dream of man.

We were disconcerted by the redemption. We liked having our sins forgiven—but how humiliating it was to see them forgiven on the cross.

We were disappointed by the resurrection. The body of Jesus was taken away. Henceforth we would have to *believe* in his presence. There would only be signs that God is among us.

How disappointed we were at the time of the ascension. He had come back, we thought, to re-establish the kingdom of Israel, and now he was going away, leaving us gaping, promising us Comfort.

The Church disappoints us too; she is too human and too divine, too complacent and too intransigent, a banner raised to rally the nations to Christ or a hobgoblin which discourages them from coming to him. But the Church is not an invention of man but of God. If she wholly satisfied us she would be untrue, for she would be ours. Happy is the man for whom the Church is the cross. He is sure to end up with God. If the Church is mysterious, disappointing, excruciating, it is because God is at work in her. Those who expect a Church which succeeds where God failed, believe neither in God nor the Church.

22

Let us prefer to suffer with all of those who suffer in her, who suffer from her. Let us pray for those who do not suffer from her: they are the worst off, for they have no cross. Let us pray for those who leave, who have given up after the first or second or third fall. The Lord, too, said and did things which were hard to accept. "Will you also go away?" (Jn. 6, 67). And they had to stay, and believe, until the day they would begin to understand.

We are disappointed by Christ's apparitions: the risen Jesus not only did not resemble God, but he no longer resembled himself! The apostles only began to recognize him when they began to *believe* that it was he who was among them.

Christ was given back to them only when they had admitted that he could manifest himself to them under any appearance whatever, with any visage whatever. Slowly, for forty days, they learned to expect him at any moment, under any circumstances, in anyone at all. The risen Christ educated them at great length: he detached them from his flesh ("the flesh is good for nothing") and attached them to his Body, which is formed of innumerable members.

* * *

The first "station" is that of Mary Magdalene and her touching despair: "They have taken away my Lord, and I do not know where they have laid him" (Jn. 20, 13).

23

This is the first thing which she understood about the resurrection (like us, about the death of those we love): she could no longer touch him, kiss him, adore him. That body to which she had been converted and purified—how she needed to see it, to wash it once more with her tears, to anoint it with her perfumes!

The resurrection affirms to us that the bodies of those we mourn will be real, but completely different. Our communication with them will be genuine, but completely different from human relations. We will be more united, but less attached.

"Mary stood weeping outside the tomb . . ." (Jn. 20, 11). She is weeping, she is alone, she has lost everything. But all that she now feels—what seems so evident—is going to be called into question. Christ urges her to believe in the supernatural world beyond: "Woman, why are you weeping? Whom do you seek?" (Jn. 20, 15).

What a strange question this is, at this moment: "Why are you weeping?" Christ seems to be astonished, innocent of what has happened and full of the freshness of a new day. Yet he still bears the traces of his terrible agony.

"She turned round and saw Jesus standing, but she did not know that it was Jesus" (Jn. 20, 14).

Jesus was present in the sadness of Mary Magdalene. Jesus is never far when we suffer. We barely complain of his absence, and he is present. We barely cry out in loneliness, and he is with us.

"Jesus said to her, 'Woman, why are you weeping? Whom

do you seek?' Supposing him to be the gardener, she said to him, 'Sir, if you have carried him away, tell me where you have laid him, and I will take him away' " (Jn. 20, 15).

A wonder: she saw Jesus, but did not recognize him! Her senses no longer served to know Jesus in the entirely new state of his risen body. He spoke, and she did not yet identify him. What is this veil between him and us? Is it inevitable that each time he shows himself to us we do not know that it is he? If Mary herself looked at him without seeing him, heard him without identifying him, how can we ever hope to recognize him when he appears before us?

"Jesus said to her, 'Mary' " (Jn. 20, 16).

He called her by her name. She heard her name pronounced as only he could pronounce it. She had recognized neither the body, nor the face, nor the voice. But this word goes to her heart. She now recognized him. She knew that this man "must" be Jesus. She rushed towards him, wanting to touch him, to grasp his knees and reassure her disoriented senses. Yet it was not only her sadness which she had to renounce, but also the source of her former joy, the way in which he had formerly been present to her. Jesus told her, "Do not hold me, for I have not yet ascended to the Father" (Jn. 20, 17). Her communication with Jesus henceforth had to be entirely spiritual. She would be able to conserve the presence of Jesus forever if she knew how to content herself with this discernment of the heart.

How she must have suffered, to renounce that so natural, so human, so sweet relationship which she had had with

25

the Lord. She could accept this new communion only little by little and by dint of strenuous belief. No doubt, this is the lesson of that mysterious phrase, "for I have not yet ascended to the Father"—that it should be related to the discourse after the Last Supper: "In a little while you will see me, because I go to the Father." Once completely glorified, spiritualized, Jesus will be accessible, visible, tangible in the sacrament of the Eucharist. The flesh of itself is of no use. Only the Spirit makes it fully significant and fully communicable.

The Lord told Mary of this new way of communicating with him, and then he said to her, "Go to the others, to my brothers." He sends her back to communicate with the others, to bring them her joy, to give what she has received.

"Mary Magdalene went and said to the disciples, 'I have seen the Lord'; and she told them that he had said these things to her" (Jn. 20, 18).

We ought to meditate on this paradox: that the only command of Christ to Magdalene, patroness of contemplatives, is: "Go to my brothers!"

Like Mary, we have to learn to recognize Jesus in quietness, in long meditation, in fervent adoration. But at the moment when we will have recognized him, when we will feel comfortably near him, he will tell us to go out to our brothers.

We can go out only when we want to stay; and we can stay in peace only if we consent to go.

We can speak only if we want to be silent; and we can be silent in peace only if we consent to speak.

It does not matter if we have an active or a contemplative inclination to begin with. The sign of God is that we will be led where we did not plan to go: active people to prayer, and contemplatives to their brothers. Then we will not have done our will, but his.

It is not the point of departure which qualifies us on the supernatural level, but the point of arrival: that we have recognized the Lord in *all* of the forms under which he presents himself to us: his word, his sacraments, his brothers.

Mary Magdalene's prayer was answered, as is every prayer, in some unanticipated way: "They have taken away my Lord, and I do not know where they have laid him . . . Tell me where you have laid him, and I will take him away."

"Go to my brethren": he is in the others! You were looking for him in the peaceful intimacy of your dialogue, and you will find him there where two or three are gathered together in his name. The gift which you give them will return to you in new grace, and you will find him waiting for you in each of those to whom you bring him.

THE DISCIPLES OF EMMAUS

GOD is word, God is apparition, God is revelation, God is love. He is nothing but love.

But we are never satisfied with the love of God. We want to see him.

In the Old Testament it was already said that "one cannot see God and live."

This is the whole moral of the apparitions: We cannot see God and continue to live as we lived before. Seeing God demands that we die to our own selves, and open our selves to *his* self, to his love.

This passage to God always lays us bare. God is the tenderest and the most terrible person in the world. The saints tell us that nothing hurts so much as the touch of God. The sign of his presence, the proof that a word of God touches us, is that we have never felt ourselves so unworthy, and that we have never been so happy. We have to die in a zone of ourselves where we are all too alive: our anxious, agitated, unconscious, sorrowful, sinful self—and we have to learn to live in a zone where we are all too dead: where God speaks, and acts, and loves us.

Let us try to make this "passage" by entering into the experiences of those who encountered him.

We are now entering the second station of joy. Let us stand still, and mark time, until the word of God has made us die and live, until it awakens us to his joy.

31

"That very day two of them were going to a village named Emmaus, about seven miles from Jerusalem, and talking with each other about all these things that had happened. While they were talking and discussing together, Jesus himself drew near and went with them. But their eyes were kept from recognizing him" (Lk. 24, 13–16).

Have you ever been to Emmaus? Have you walked along the road there in solitude, ruminating, wondering about the past? Did you not recognize the one who walked beside you?

"And he said to them, 'What is this conversation which you are holding with each other as you walk?'" (Lk. 24, 17).

This is God's reproach to men: How heavy with your own thoughts you are! How dull you are!

The disciples of Emmaus had believed that they had *seen*. They were discouraged and sad because they believed that Jesus was dead, and that they were now alone.

Let us measure the difference: they were sad because they believed that he was dead—and we are sad even though we believe that he is alive!

Is our faith in the resurrection of Christ, in his ascension, in his sitting at the right hand of the Father, tantamount to believing that he is dead?

Like the disciples of Emmaus, we must undergo the experience of an *encounter* with "a certain Jesus, who was dead, but whom Paul asserted to be alive" (Acts 25, 19). Like them, we will have to acknowledge that God has fulfilled our hope ("We had hoped that he was the one to redeem Israel . . ."), but not in the way we had foreseen.

"Then one of them, named Cleophas, answered him, 'Are you the only visitor to Jerusalem who does not know?'"

Cleophas is impatient with this man who cannot perceive his sorrow. He is ready to furnish his list, to enumerate his good reasons for his sorrow.

But the Christian is the man of thanksgiving. He enumerates his motives for thanks and gratitude. When he goes to Mass, it is not to complain, to implore graces, but to give thanks!

The dialogue of the hidden Christ with the disciples of Emmaus is renewed at every Mass: What are you sad about? Jesus asks. Why are you depressed? Why are you not celebrating the Eucharist?

And like the wayfarers we answer, "Do you not know what I have been going through?" Then Jesus amazes us with his answer "What have you been going through?", he asks us.

Will we ever understand this kind of innocence of God, this dazzling amazement, what Claudel called "the eternal childhood of God"? When we speak to Christ of his terrible passion, or when we want to remind him of the awful events which we have endured, he gives us the impression of having so perfectly passed into the joy and the glory of his Father that he can scarcely remember the terrible way which led him there.

33

The disciples began to understand, in the light of the Scriptures, what had happened, what they had witnessed, what they had taken part in, without having understood anything. They saw how slow to believe they had been, how close-minded and blind, how taken up with themselves. God had been constantly with them, and they had not realized it.

"And beginning with Moses"—which means the books of Moses, that is to say, *Genesis*—"and all the prophets" (Lk. 24, 27), he explained to them how the presence of God had been manifested to men since the beginning of history. Our refusal to recognize him only provoked him to goodness. He gave us remedies for our miseries, and answers to our objections. He repaid our ingratitude with love, and he promised us resurrection after death.

Little by little the apostles came to realize that the presence of God through the whole history of the world had reached its climax, the high point of its manifestation, before their eyes, at the very moment when they believed they were most lost, most abandoned!

They were awakened, overthrown; they let themselves be worked upon by the word of God. "Blessed are those who hear the word of God and keep it!" They did not yet recognize Christ, but because of his interpretation of the Scriptures they act as though they had.

It is efficient, the word of God! The apostles allowed themselves to be led by it and they obeyed it: "Stay with us, for it is toward evening . . ." (Lk. 24, 29).

They are like the just, who on the day of judgment will

ask, "Lord, when did we see thee hungry and feed thee, or thirsty and give thee drink?" (Mt. 25, 37). Jesus will answer, "You obeyed a sure instinct, you opened yourselves to grace, you started living according to faith when you acted towards your brothers as you would have towards me, if you had known me."

Charity led the disciples of Emmaus to complete faith, as it does with all the "anonymous" Christians of the pagan world who love, without naming him, Jesus hidden in the least of his brothers. But as for us, we who call ourselves Christians—does our faith ever lead us to this charity?

"So they drew near to the village to which they were going. He appeared to be going further. . . ."

Jesus does not want to impose himself upon us, but always leaves it to us to request his company. He wants us to act freely. And it is easy for us to act as though we have not heard him or recognized him, so that we are spared the trouble of asking him in.

God is humble. He is in our midst as our servant, patiently and silently waiting our command. Each of us has this terrible power of consigning him to perpetual silence.

". . . but they constrained him, saying, 'Stay with us, for it is towards evening and the day is now far spent.' So he went in to stay with them."

No one is more docile than Christ. No one is so readily available to heed our wishes. He is faithful always.

"When he was at table with them, he took the bread and blessed, and broke it, and gave it to them. And their eyes were opened and they recognized him; and he vanished out of their sight. They said to each other, 'Did not our hearts burn within us while he talked to us on the road, while he opened to us the Scriptures?" (Lk. 24, 30–32).

How do you understand this text? Do you think that Jesus changed suddenly, that he took on again his old appearance?

If that were the case, then the apostles must not have changed, they were able to recognize God through their senses. And if they recognized him as flesh and blood, then they must have remained themselves merely flesh and blood, and therefore strangers to the kingdom of God. No, something completely different happened.

When the apostles were at table with this unknown guest, who held such sway over their hearts, who spoke of the Scriptures with such authority, they watched him take bread —with the authority of their Master. They had the sudden feeling that they had already lived through the event which was now taking place, that what was now happening had taken place not so many days before. They were trying desperately to remember. And then they looked at him again, and they were able to recognize with their eyes the one whom they had already recognized in their hearts. Jesus then became invisible to their eyes. The apparition vanished, and what remained on the table was the bread, the visible sign of his living presence in their souls.

The apostles recognized Jesus only through faith. They recognized him in his sacrament, by his gesture of love—

sharing the bread. They recognized him through this gift of themselves which he succeeded in bringing forth from them. He led them first to invite him in, to treat him as a brother, and then he brought them to believe in the presence within them and among them of something sacred and divine which asserted itself from the moment they had confidence in their belief.

The disciples of Emmaus made an act of faith as we do. Newman said that here the Lord went from the hiding-place of seeing without knowing, to that of knowing without seeing.

Our Lord was not playing some kind of trick on the apostles which would make their task more difficult and thus more "commendable." God has a hard enough time as it is making himself recognized. But he wants to be recognized only through his love. God speaks to our hearts. Only those who listen to him in their heart truly know him, and respect what is most loving and intimate in him—his love.

If the disciples at Emmaus had recognized Christ merely by looking at him, they would not really have known him. They would have remained without understanding and slow to believe. They would not have become sensitive and docile in the presence of God.

But fortunately the disciples recognized their Lord— in the same ways that we are given to recognize him: in his living word, and in the breaking of the bread. In fact, almost every apparition of Christ was accompanied by a meal. The apostles learned to recognize him at Mass.

Further, our Lord's apparition to the disciples at Emmaus ended with a sending. "Go," he told them, "the Mass is ended." At Emmaus he told them that "repentance and forgiveness of sins should be preached in [my] name to all nations." Then he left them, and the disciples went immediately to find the others. They did not stay to give thanks. They wanted to rush to the others to communicate to them their joy and their faith. Like Mary Magdalene, they were sent into the apostolate and the fraternal life. They went from the Head to the members, from the eucharistic body to the ecclesial body.

"And they rose that same hour and returned to Jerusalem; and they found the eleven gathered together and those who were with them, who said, 'The Lord has risen indeed, and has appeared to Simon!' Then they told what had happened on the road, and how he was known to them in the breaking of the bread" (Lk. 24, 33–35).

Their joy was to make the primitive Church understand that the presence of Christ was not some fugitive apparition, a stroke of luck on their part, an extraordinary coincidence. Their eucharistic experience proved to them that it was the right of each believer to recognize the presence of God within them, by the power confided to them in God's living word and bread. Now all of them would be able to gather together fraternally and celebrate the Eucharist, to make Jesus present among them in the breaking of the bread.

The apostles now lacked nothing in the world, for from the moment when he became invisible to their eyes, they chose to recognize him in their hearts.

* * *

Joy is slow to stir in us! The disciples of Emmaus had to walk for miles with the Lord before their hearts had warmed sufficiently to recognize him. But let us not reproach them, for those who are too quickly joyous will not have their joy for very long.

Father Faber has said, "Some lives seem from afar like gigantic peaks which look down on humanity, but one should not forget that those heights, those mountains, those summits only reveal the secret upheavals of suffering. Convulsions, cataclysms raised them that high!"

Our joy must be in proportion to our suffering. It is our sorrow which must be turned into joy. The apostles seem very slow and heavy, our Lord had constantly to repeat things to them, yet they would answer, "We understand nothing. Explain it to us again. . . ." They had to be convinced at great length. But their faith was as sincere as their former incredulity, their joy as profound as their former despair.

For too many of us, religion consists in pretending to believe ourselves to be somewhat lost. There is then only one solution: to pretend to believe ourselves to be somewhat saved. But true religion is outside of these two hypocrisies.

39

The true religion of redemption says that only the lost are saved. "Now the tax collectors and sinners were all drawing near to hear him. And the Pharisees and the Scribes murmured, saying, 'This man receives sinners and eats with them!'" (Lk. 15, 1–2). This was the company of our Lord. We are good Christians only if we admit that we are sinners. And our joy at Mass should be the joy of all sinners whom the Lord receives at his table.

Christianity is not optimistic. Chesterton said that the optimist is a happy idiot and the pessimist an unhappy idiot. We are neither optimistic nor pessimistic. We believe in the redemption of the world, but through the remission of sins. We believe that man is a sinner and that God forgives. We believe that man does evil, but that God is so good that he forgives him. We believe that God is the one who transforms each of our faults into happy faults—faults which reveal the goodness and tenderness of God. "Those who are well have no need of a physician, but those who are sick" (Mt. 9, 12).

True joy is slowly attained by degrees. We need only meditate on the life of the mother of our Lord to know the nature of true joy. Her words are a great source of comfort for us. "And when they saw him they were astonished; and his mother said to him, 'Son, why have you treated us so?'" (Lk. 2, 48). "And they did not understand the saying which he spoke to them" (Lk. 2, 50). These are refreshing words, realistic words, and they help us to understand that Mary's joy, too, was a sorrow surmounted, a joy of faith.

Joy is not necessarily exuberant or sentient. It is a joy *in faith*. But it is as genuine and living as our faith.

We have an inexhaustible joy, but it proceeds from a perpetual miracle; it is a daily gift of the Father, as is our faith, our hope, our charity.

We should recall to mind daily this beautiful passage of St. Peter: "Always be prepared to make a defense to any one who calls you to account for the hope that is in you" (1 Pet. 3, 15).

* * *

The first joy, the first beatitude which the disciples of Emmaus heard, is expressed this way: "Blessed are those who hear the word of God!"

It is the word of God which created us. "God spoke, and it was done . . ." Each of us has been called into existence by a word of God, each of us is a living word of God who must edify. We began to exist only because God pronounced our name. And every time he pronounces it again we experience a new birth, our life is renewed, our heart awakens, our joy rises, and we feel as if we have not lived until then.

The people of God, the Church, are constituted by a call, a word of God which brings them together, and that is why this word is proclaimed at the beginning of each of our

41

Christian assemblies. It is the word of God which creates and holds together the people of God.

It is also the word of God which will judge us. God himself will not judge us. "The Father judges no one, . . ."—the Father is not a judge, he is a Father—"he has given all judgment to the Son" (Jn. 5, 22). And the Son does not judge anyone—"For I did not come to judge the world but to save the world" (Jn. 12, 47).

Neither the Father nor the Son will judge us. They are love, help, pity, call, forgiveness, mercy; they are not judges.

God has told us that his word will be our judge. "If anyone hears my sayings and does not keep them, I do not judge him; for I did not come to judge the world but to save the world. He who rejects me and does not receive my sayings has a judge; the word that I have spoken will be his judge on the last day" (Jn. 12, 47–49).

The judgment will be decided on these questions: "Did the word of God speak to you? Did the word of God heal you? Did the word of God bear fruit in you? Did you hear the word of God and keep it?"

It will be the word of God which will raise us. "The hour is coming, and now is, when the dead will hear the voice of the Son of God, and those who will hear will live" (Jn. 5, 25). The word of God can raise the dead! And there is always in each of us a resurrection to be done, a dead inert zone to be brought to life again.

Before reading the word of God, we should kneel and

pray. "Without me you can do nothing." No one can hear a word of God by himself. "He who listens to a prophecy needs the same grace as he who proffers it," the Fathers of the Church used to say. The Spirit who inspired the book must inspire the reader. Each word of the Scriptures, in order not to remain a dead letter, must be taken up again, invaded again, charged with meaning again by the breath of the Spirit of God who brings dead bones back to life.

"For the word of God is living," St. Paul says (Heb. 4, 12). It is living, efficient, sharper than a two-edged sword, piercing, disentangling the feelings and the thoughts of our heart. It has a lot of work to do in each of us.

When we break the eucharistic bread, we do not unite with the Christ living two thousand years ago, we communicate with Christ present. When we open the Gospel we do not read what happened once upon a time, but listen to Jesus Christ who is speaking—to us.

We must listen to his word, and meditate upon it. To meditate upon the word means this: to repeat it to oneself until it speaks. This takes a long time.

In confronting the word of God, there are two foolish attitudes. The first is to say, "It's marvelous, I've understood everything. How clear it is! It's luminous!" The other is, "I don't understand anything. It's discouraging. Let's close the book. It doesn't teach me anything."

Between the two, there is only one right attitude, that of Mary: "And they did not understand the saying which he spoke to them . . . but she kept all these things in her heart." Do you know any other way of hearing the word of God than Mary's way?

* * *

Our Orthodox brothers do not expose the Blessed Sacrament on the altar. Rather, they enthrone on the altar the book of the Gospel, and surround it with candles. We can take communion only once a day, but we can listen to God as often as we want. He is always speaking to us. Man does not live by bread alone, even by the eucharistic bread, but he lives by every word which comes from the mouth of God.

Let us suppose that someone was curious to taste unleavened bread, and by mistake ate a consecrated host. He would not thereby commit a sacrilege, but on the other hand he would not receive communion either. He did not receive any grace, for he took the host to be ordinary bread—and for him it was ordinary bread.

In the same way, if we read the Gospel as an ordinary book, if we regard it without veneration or faith, it is for us an ordinary book. We will receive no grace from reading it.

Christ himself was only an ordinary man for all those who approached him without faith, who regarded him as only an ordinary man. But the sick woman in the crowd approached Christ with faith, saying to herself, "If I only touch his garment, I shall be made well" (Mt. 9, 21). Jesus is surrounded and pressed upon by so many curious people that she cannot come near him. But she threads her way, and at last she reaches him and touches him—and an immense well-being pervades her body. She is healed! At once Christ stops. He asks, "Who was it that touched me?" (Lk. 8, 45).

The apostles, realists as usual, answer, "How should we know? Everyone is pushing up against us. If only they would give us some room!"

But Christ does not pay any attention to them. "Some one touched me," he says again, "for I perceive that power has gone forth from me" (Lk. 8, 46).

Then the apostles realize that something serious has just happened. Each one steps back, apologizes, defends himself: "*I* didn't do anything. I didn't touch you." But the poor woman, seeing that she has been found out, falls on her knees trembling, and declares that she was the one who touched him, and had been healed.

Christ says to her, "Daughter, your faith has made you well, go in peace" (Lk. 8, 48).

Everyone is touching him, everybody is pressing upon him. No one is healed. Only one person touches him with respect, with faith, with love, and she is transformed, renewed, healed.

* * *

What does it mean, to read the Gospel with faith?

If we read it as a history book, then we regard it as an ordinary book. But the Gospel is much more than history.

It is prophecy and revelation. The Gospel is a light for our life, for every life. It helps us to recognize the presence of God among us. It is the word of God among us.

The Gospel is God coming to live among men. "I am with you always." But, as always, God does not impose himself upon us. He lets us follow the example of the sick woman, who seeks him out. He calls to us, he speaks, but it is so easy for us not to pay any attention.

The Gospel is a mirror, and the function of a mirror, as we know, is to show us the image of ourselves.

In the Gospel we are predicted, foretold, denounced. The Gospel reveals how God acts towards us, and how we act towards him. "Father, forgive them, for they know not what they do."

The Gospel is a revelation, and we must in faith let ourselves be revealed in it.

Of course, we are rather expert in seeing everyone else reflected in the Gospel. We are indignant, for instance, about the incredulity of the Jews. We find it hard to believe that they did not recognize the presence of the Saviour among them.

In the parable of the sower, do we consider ourselves like the stony ground upon which the seed falls, or like the thorns, or are we like the good soil where the seed can be fertile, life-giving, and efficacious?

The word of God not only reveals, it also acts. It illuminates and transforms. It is sacramentally efficacious. Every week we solemnly assemble to participate in the efficacy of a single word of God. The true word of the Mass is not the reading of the epistle and the gospel. These are a preparation for, an orientation towards the central mystery. The true word of the Mass is spoken at the moment of consecration.

At the moment of consecration a word is spoken with faith and listened to with faith, and it takes on the efficacy it had when it was first spoken. By a word, bread is transformed—transubstantiated. And before we receive this bread we kneel and say, "Lord, say but a word and my soul will be healed."

Is it true? Has he ever said a word, have we ever discovered a word which has healed us? We must ask ourselves this terrible question often, and thereby accept the judgment of the word—so that we will not one day be condemned by it.

*　*　*

The disciples at Emmaus recognized Christ both in his word and in the breaking of the bread. We have already remarked that the risen Christ appeared to his disciples almost every time during a meal. He initiated them to the celebration of the Eucharist. He prepared them to recognize him in a daily apparition, when they were to assemble and break bread in memory of their Lord.

The disciples of Emmaus found Christ in his gesture of love and giving by which he shared his bread. The bread is what maintains life. Who gives his bread gives his life. They recognized him in his gesture of love by which he was giving his life, in this greatest love which God alone has.

Do we recognize God by his love? Do we realize how immeasurable his love is?

What convinces us more: a miracle, or the Eucharist; a manifestation of power, or a sign of pure love?

When God revealed himself, when he wanted to manifest himself, and to show how we should think of him, he did not try to impress us, or dazzle us. He appeared as a child, an innocent, fragile being, delivered up and offered. Later he was crucified, hung on the wood. Finally he took the form of bread. He wanted to appear in the midst of us as someone who serves, as the last of all and as the servant of all.

When his hour had come, the hour of his true revelation, Christ made no more miracles. He died on the cross. He revealed the humanity of God, the weakness of God, the suffering of God, the love of God. He crucified his power.

"Now you have to be strong with my strength," he says, "joyful with my joy, for I have nothing else to give you." We can hardly come to the crucified Lord and ask for favors—for success, protection, power. He has taught us how to give our life away, how to serve. If we want success or protection or power, we will have to ask the devil.

God is weak in this world, but there is no greater strength than to dare to be weak as a child and servant.

Do we believe in God's love? Do we recognize Jesus Christ in the breaking of the eucharistic bread? We have so often shared this bread of Christ—but have we ever thus been led to share ours? Have we invited to our table those with whom we approached the table of the Lord? Has the sacrament of the Eucharist—the sign of love and sharing—ever led us to the reality it signifies? Has Christ's sacrifice ever been good for anything except to take the place of ours?

God is for everyone—but everyone is for himself. With everyone else we go to communion, we eat the same bread, we say the same prayers, we sing the same thanksgiving. We share God, but nothing else.

And yet Christ told us, "Do this in memory of me." If we recognized Christ in the gesture of love through which he shares his bread, his life, it is up to us to make him known today, to reveal him still living through his love which urges us to give our bread and our life.

"See how they love one another," Tertullian said of the early Christians. Would that observation be valid today? Is Christ visible in our midst when we celebrate together the eucharistic act of love and union?

The sacrament is a sign—sensible sign. Christ wanted the sacrament to be a visible manifestation of invisible grace. The sacraments give grace, they make us Christ-like.

* * *

The place where we worship God is not so important as how we worship him, and we are to worship God in spirit and in truth. All Christians are delegated by their baptism to join the worshiping assembly. We are called to consecrate, sanctify, and divinize the world, filling it with love.

When we celebrate the Mass we are giving momentary expression to what is or should be a constant activity of ours —the sanctification and consecration of the world. The celebration gives us strength, the Eucharist is the sign and source of this world-divinization; but it is strength and sign and source only if we understand it to be so.

We celebrate the true Mass in our home or in our work; true thanksgiving is done "at all times and in all places." When we leave the Christian assembly we go out into all those secular "churches" that make up the world.

Yet very few of us are aware of our real professional and familial vocation—that of being a priest of God. Very few of us realize how much we have to give thanks for. Of course, we love our life, our work, our family, our neighborhood. But we complain a lot as well. We cannot accept and give thanks to God for the trials he has sent us. We have no more respect for the will of God than we have for our work.

How can we solemnly gather to thank God each Sunday when during the week we have refused what he has offered to us? How can we gather to celebrate the Eucharist in the assembly, when we do not celebrate it anywhere else? If the Eucharist is not a sign of our priestly vocation, how can it be an effective source of strength?

Our mission is to fill the world with the charity of Christ, to transform the world into a place where peace and justice reign and where people love one another. This is the true sacerdotal work, this is the true sacrificial mission.

The world is redeemed in our lives, not on the altars of churches. We will sanctify the world only through the intensity of our faith and in the love which we put into our life.

Let us imagine that the priest is about to offer the host at the altar, and that this host is made from bread which during the week *we* earned and kneaded ourselves. What kind of bread is the priest going to consecrate? What taste will it have? How terrible it would be if we offered to God, for him to become incarnate in, a bread of hate, bitterness, complaint, rancor, disgust. Will it be the bread of justice and honesty, a bread of love of our brothers, a bread joyfully kneaded in respect for the mission which has been entrusted to us?

This bread is a sign of our lives. A sign must signify something, and if this bread is corrupt it cannot signify anything other than corruption. If it is corrupt it cannot be consecrated, because God does not want it. This bread can be consecrated and will be accepted only if it is a sign of our love for God and our brothers. On this condition only can it be a source of strength for us.

We are responsible for transforming the world into a state of grace, for offering it to God as a host-sign of our love for him. The world should end in a Eucharist. The Fathers of the Church used to say, "When the Eucharist will be validly celebrated throughout the world, then the world will pass away." The world will then have made the passage, the passover, to the Lord, for it will have been offered and conse-crated to him.

How beautiful it would be: the whole world united in thanksgiving, offering to God the bread which men have earned and shared. They would adore Christ in the uni-versal breaking of the bread.

THE THIRD STATION

PETER

THIS is the most beautiful station, a story of open air, cool wind, the sun rising above the sea.

"After this Jesus revealed himself again to the disciples by the Sea of Tiberias; and he revealed himself in this way. Simon Peter, Thomas called the Twin, Nathanael of Cana in Galilee, the sons of Zebedee, and two others of his disciples were together. Simon Peter said to them, 'I am going fishing.' They said to him, 'We will go with you'" (Jn. 21, 1–3).

As with us, the religious life of the apostles began to slacken after the resurrection. The emotional torpor of the days and weeks before had exhausted them, and now they wanted rest and relief. They began to take up their old, re-assuring jobs as fisherman. But the Lord had told them that now they had new and more important and much more difficult work to do. "I will make you fishers of men" (Mk. 4, 19).

"But that night they caught nothing. Just as the day was breaking, Jesus stood on the beach; yet the disciples did not know it was Jesus" (Jn. 21, 3–4).

Always the Lord is present. We are never alone. He asked them whether they had caught any fish—for he is concerned with their problems, and knows how tired and disheartened they must be. But they can only answer no. This is earth's answer to heaven.

Like Mary Magdalene, the apostles did not know it was

55

Jesus. Like her, they were in tears, for they had spent the whole night casting their nets and had not caught anything.

"He said to them, 'Cast the net on the right side of the boat, and you will find some.'"

They cast their net, and were not able to haul it in because of the weight of the fish.

"That disciple whom Jesus loved said to Peter, 'It is the Lord!'" (Jn. 21, 6-7).

The disciples did not recognize Jesus—not even after they had seen and heard him. Only John, the most sensitive of the apostles, felt in his heart the old emotion. He felt that someone was near whom he loved, and finally it came to him: "It is the Lord!" It could only have been the Lord!

When was the last time we were alone, when we were afraid, when we fretted and worried?

"When Simon Peter heard that it was the Lord, he put on his clothes, for he was stripped for work, and sprang into the sea. But the other disciples came in the boat, dragging the net full of fish ... When they got out on land, they saw a charcoal fire there, with fish lying on it, and bread" (Jn. 21, 7-9).

Christ was serving them a meal. His first words to them were, "Come and have breakfast" (Jn. 21, 12).

Jesus was being perfectly natural. He smiled at them, and invited them to join him. But the apostles were full of haphazard emotion—fear, uncertainty, joy. There next follows the most beautiful sentence of the Johannine Gospel: "Now none of the disciples dared to ask him, 'Who are you?' They knew it was the Lord" (21, 12).

These are wonderful words, full of grace and meaning and mystery and comfort. They are words that can be said of each of us.

In a certain way, somehow deep within them, the apostles knew that it was the Lord—that it could only have been the Lord. They were convinced of that fact independently of what they saw—or rather, of what they did not see, for Jesus was no longer as he was when they knew him.

The senses rebel against this kind of inner conviction. The apostles wanted to touch and hear their Master, to be given evidence of this radiant presence. They wanted a word of affirmation: "Yes, it is I." But they refrained from asking him who he was, and the more they renounced this capricious desire, the more their certainty grew—the more they knew that it could only have been the Lord.

If the apostles had given way to doubt, they would never have been able to be certain. If they had demanded evidence, they would never have believed.

How is it with us? When Christ appears to us—in his word and in the eucharistic bread—do we doubt that it is he? When he manifests himself to us, do we recognize his presence? Do we dare ask, "Who are you?"

When their education was complete, the apostles knew that the Lord was everywhere, that he could appear at any moment—and often where he was least expected. They became prudent, attentive, respected—and they recognized him unceasingly.

This, then, is our choice: either to complain of not meeting him anywhere, or to rejoice in meeting him at every turn.

* * *

Like the others, this apparition and this meal terminate with Jesus sending his disciples on a mission.

"When they had finished breakfast, Jesus said to Simon Peter, 'Simon, son of John, do you love me more than these?' He said to him, 'Yes, Lord; you know that I love you.' He said to him, 'Feed my lambs'" (Jn. 21, 15).

Peter was sent out to his brothers. Like his Lord and Master, he was to live and serve others, to unite himself with them. He was to prepare for them the eucharistic meal, and eat it together with them. "Feed my lambs."

Peter is charged with responsibility for the Church; he is vested with service in regard to the members of Christ. He is servant of the servants of God. He should always be the first to recognize his Lord in the least of his own.

The meal ends with Jesus prophesying the destiny of Peter; he was also prophesying the destiny of each of us.

" 'Truly, truly, I say to you, when you were young, you girded yourself and walked where you would; but when you are old, you will stretch out your hands, and another will gird you and carry you where you do not wish to go.'

(This he said to show by what death he was to glorify God.)" (Jn. 21, 18–19).

When he was young, Peter did his own will; he wanted a redemption without the cross, an apparition without pain, a kingdom of comfort.

When we are young, we too like always to have our own way. We like to live as we please, according to our whims. But to be an adult in Christ is to accept to do the will of another, to accept the real apparition of God in our lives, which does not take place according to our good pleasure.

Do you live now according to your own will, or have you submitted yourself to the will of another? Do you go where you want? Do you do what you want? Then you are still very young. But when you are adult in Christ, then another —then several others—will have taken you by the hand and will have led you where you did not want to go, where you would never have had the courage to go, but where you will be proud and happy to have been so well led.

"This he said to show by what death he was to glorify God." This death was death to self.

Peter's whole life, like each of our lives, like each of the apparitions, is the story of an old prayer answered.

One day, on Mount Tabor, Peter had said to his Master, "Lord, we are glad that we are here. Why can we not set up our tents here, and stay forever?"

And Christ gave a mysterious answer which implied death and resurrection, passion and joy.

And one day on *his* cross where he did not want to go,

Peter said what he had said on Mount Tabor: "Lord, I am glad to be here. I thank you for having led me here. It is so much more beautiful than what I wanted. Now I am willing to stay."

And you, where do you stand? On Mount Tabor? Then do not speak of destiny until you have gone through death and resurrection.

But if you are at Calvary, if you are in the place where you did not want to go, where you have been led by gentle hands, by a call of the Lord, then say on your Calvary what you said one day on the Mount Tabor of a retreat, of a prayer, of a vocation, of a marriage: "Lord, I am glad I am here. It is good after all to be where you wanted me to be. I am willing to set up my tent here, and stay forever."

THOMAS

LET us continue our pilgrimage on the way of joy by standing still and being patient! Let us be humble enough to recognize that we too are foolish and slow to believe. Just as we meditate, during Lent, before each station of the way of the cross in order to try to pity, to sympathize, to identify ourselves with the suffering Christ, thus and perhaps even more we need to halt, to stand at each station of the way of joy in order to let ourselves be filled with the certainty of the presence, of the love, of the joy of the risen Christ.

The fourth station is that of Thomas. It is the one that the Church keeps for the Sunday after Easter, at the end of the week of the apparitions, for those who would not yet be convinced. As a last chance to convert us to joy, to convince us of the resurrection, the Church chooses the argument of that disciple whom we most resemble: the resister, the doubter, the pessimist, someone who had growled a long time that he would not give way, that he would not let himself believe, that he would not be had so easily! Thomas is hard-headed. He held out longer than the others, he was a skeptical realist who was mistrustful when things looked too good.

Thomas, like us moderns, believed only in what he touched. He was a man who wanted to have no illusions; he was a courageous pessimist who was willing to face evil, but who did not dare to believe in happiness. For him, the worst was always the surest.

Thomas's character is outlined several times in the Gospel, and always in the same way.

At the resurrection of Lazarus, someone came to tell Jesus, "Lord, he whom you love is ill" (a discreet and confident prayer; he asks nothing, but notifies the Lord, and waits). The disciples worried about the danger of going to Judaea, but Jesus reassured them in a mysterious sentence which affirmed to them that they were not in danger. Then "Thomas, called the Twin, said to his fellow disciples, 'Let us also go, that we may die with him'" (Jn. 11, 16).

This was not, of course, a word of faith, but of despair. Thomas rudely contradicted the Lord. He had courage enough only to die, but not to be confident. This same pessimism led him to reject so vigorously the announcement of the resurrection.

At another time, Jesus said, "'When I go and prepare a place for you, I will come again and will take you to myself, that where I am you may be also. And you know the way where I am going.' Thomas said to him, 'Lord, we do not know where you are going; how can we know the way?'" (Jn. 14, 3–6).

It is with this flat intervention that he interrupts the beautiful discourse after the Last Supper. Jesus answers him in his mysterious and transparent fashion: "I am the way, and the truth, and the life . . ." (Jn. 14, 6). Still, Thomas could not find his bearings; no doubt, on hearing these words of Jesus, he grumbled to himself, "With this kind of information we're sure to go far!"

Finally, there is Thomas's amazing final stubbornness: "Unless I see in his hands the print of the nails, and place my finger in the marks of the nails, and place my hand in his side, I will not believe" (Jn. 20, 25).

Yet there is something about Thomas, the violence of his revolt, the hateful conditions he set for his surrender, which makes us sympathize with him. His terrible hardness could have come only from terrible suffering. It was because he suffered more than all of the others that he no longer wanted to take the risk of hoping. Thomas was probably the one who suffered the most from the passion, who most regretted not having been able to die as well. He had only one stone to rest his head upon—despair. At least this rock was well embedded and not easily pried loose.

Have not we also tried too often to believe, with no other result than to have exposed ourselves to cruel disappointments? We are tempted to say, "Let me go no further. I want to withdraw. The pain is too much." Such was Thomas's spirit: an exasperated suffering.

There are many brave men who are capable of facing suffering and death. Two world wars have given us enough proof of that. Wars have shown us that men can even be cynical and blasé in face of imminent death. But are there very many men today who are not afraid to open themselves to hope and happiness, who are not afraid to shed their armor of distrust and resignation?

Today men like to believe in nothing and yet do their duty as men. There is something in this attitude which is at once both beautiful and childish. He who pretends no longer to have hope, hopes not to hope any longer. He who pretends to believe in nothing, believes that he does not believe.

To suffer from not loving someone is the sign of genuine love. To suffer from not being able to believe, from not being able to hope, is the form of faith in our time—a discreet, humble, tragic, excruciating faith, but one that is sincere, honest, and pure.

Fortunately, the Lord knew Thomas well. Only the Lord knew that it was because he had been hurt so much that Thomas had become so skeptical. Only the Lord knew that in order to cure him it was necessary to comfort him.

Thomas's demands were concrete and almost materialistic in character. "Unless I see in his hands the print of the nails, and place my fingers in the mark of the nails, and place my hand in his side, . . ." Like us, he had a great fear of letting himself be fooled. What a relief it must have been to him to have found himself so well predicted—so wrong! We are like Thomas in that our religious life, too, will not change unless we are given staisfaction. Seeing and touching the divine—recognizing the presence of God—helps our faith to become impassioned, enthusiastic, and alive.

God's answer to Thomas's demand was overwhelming, incredible, disarming. It surpassed all that he could ever have imagined or hoped for. What Thomas had expressed as a flippant challenge in the impassioned fury of his resistance to believe, Jesus now takes him up on. "Come Thomas, put your finger, put your hand . . . and do not be faithless but believing." The Lord let himself be defeated by Thomas. To accommodate Thomas he had to abandon the plan which he used for all of the others. For Thomas alone Jesus changed his method. But in this way he saved Thomas.

Thomas had resisted the authority of the entire apostolic college. He was the first protestant. But had he been a mere conformist, had he thrown in his lot with the others simply in order not to make trouble, he would have become a very mediocre Christian, he would never have said, "My Lord and my God." He was led by strange ways. By protesting he came to affirm. No doubt, the apostles were so exasperated by his stubbornness that they were almost ready to pressure him into believing. But the Lord loved Thomas. He knew that if he proved so stubborn, it was because he had been so unhappy, he knew that no one was more generous. —"Let us also go," Thomas had said, unbelieving but also unselfish, "that we may die with him."

The doors were shut and the apostles were alone, but Jesus appeared among them. He greeted them, and then he said to Thomas, "Put your finger here, and see my hands; and put out your hand, and place it in my side; do not be faithless, but believing" (Jn. 20, 27).

Thomas was entirely overwhelmed, for he had never believed that his wish would be answered. His challenge had been a refusal, a means of shutting himself up in his doubt, of setting himself apart from this irritating band of gullible believers—of excommunicating himself.

The Lord, by his gentleness, reconciled Thomas immediately. Thomas touched the living proof of all the love with which he had been loved. He touched, and collapsed in tears before his Lord.

When Thomas saw the Lord before him, radiating peace and love, he suddenly understood that he had known all along that Jesus was risen. He had always known that it could only have been so. He had had enough experience, he had lived long enough with Jesus to know that he had to expect it, that with Jesus it was always the unexpected and incredible which happened.

Thomas should have believed the others. By refusing, he only mortified himself, martyred himself—to secure himself against a later terrible blow. He was dying with both desire and fear of believing.

There was no worse punishment for Thomas than to obtain what he had set as the condition of his faith. He saw that he had missed his chance, that he, too, should have given his faith to the Lord.

Now Thomas no longer wanted to touch the wounds of the Lord; he would have given anything not to hear the gentle reproach: "Because you have seen, Thomas, you have believed. Blessed are those who have not seen and yet believe." Before Jesus spoke, Thomas must have thought of

it, looking at the others who had had the happiness of believing.

When Thomas actually touched his Lord, it was with
docility and repentance. Touching the Lord was the most
painful and humiliating thing which Thomas could have
done. He was making reparation.

But Thomas was also transported to heights of joy where
no one had ever been before. By Jesus' intimate revelation of
his love, Thomas came to know "the breadth and length and
height and depth" (Eph. 3, 18) of this love of Christ which
surpasses all understanding. Thomas fell to his knees and
said, "My Lord and my God." He was the first to have
pushed the faith that far. No apostle had yet called Jesus his
God.

From doubting Thomas, Jesus drew the most beautiful act
of faith in the Gospel. Jesus loved him so well, healed him
so gently, that from this fault, this bitterness, this humiliation, Jesus brought forth a joyful affirmation. God alone
knows how to make our faults become happy faults—faults
which remind us only of the marvelous kindness which was
revealed by God when he forgave them.

Thomas *thought* he did not believe. We too are often
more faithful, more believing, than we think. The proof of
our belief is that we are so unhappy thinking that we do not
believe. Blessed are those who are unhappy in their unbelief!
Nothing so moves the Lord to act as desperate resistance to
him. "Blessed are those who have not seen," the Lord said,
"and yet believe." He said these words for us.

Therefore, let us not ask to see the wounds of the Lord and to touch them with our hand. Now in the time of resurrection we have the passion behind us. The risen Lord is waiting for us to join him, and he will refuse us nothing so that we may be with him. If we are obstinate, Jesus will manifest himself to us—and then, in humiliation, we will be forced to recognize his presence. On that day when we see God we will know that our greatest fault was to have doubted that we would ever see him.

The story of Thomas is also the story of a prayer heard; but whereas the others—Mary Magdalene, the disciples on the way to Emmaus, Peter—did not realize that their prayer had been answered, Thomas did. He received what he had demanded, and now he did not want it.

Let us pray confidently, therefore, for one day our un-heard prayer will also be answered.

* * *

The disciples of Emmaus recognized Christ by his word and by the breaking of the bread. But Thomas recognized him by his forgiveness. Thus we are now going to spend some time meditating on the encounter with Christ in the sacrament of forgiveness, for our understanding of joy will not be complete unless we also understand and experience the joy of penitence. This is a paradox only for those who do not know what we mean.

Penitence is not remorse, not even sorrow for having

sinned; rather, it is a conversion, a renewal—it is a turning towards the true God who calls us, full of kindness and mercy. True penitence takes place only in a dialogue where there is no anguish, with a God so kind that, far from fearing his chastisements, we are afraid only of hurting him.

It is before the true God that we see ourselves as sinners. We do not know what we are lacking until it has been given back to us. It is upon leaving the confessional that we discover what we should have accused ourselves of. The worst mutilation is the one we remain unconscious of.

When the true God appears to us, then and only then do we know ourselves as sinners—unconscious, ungrateful, indifferent, rebellious. Only the kindness of his forgiveness allows us to bear the revelation of our faults.

The greatest joy is truly to be forgiven. It is perhaps not the greatest joy on earth, but it is the greatest joy in heaven. "There will be more joy in heaven," our Lord has said, "over one sinner who repents than over ninety-nine righteous persons who need no repentance. . . . There is joy before the angels of God over one sinner who repents" (Lk. 15, 7. 10).

We do not celebrate penitence any more. It has become the saddest of the sacraments—and the most degraded. Forgiveness has become a hurried receipt. Yet the good news of the Gospel, the joyful message which we are responsible for announcing to the world, is that sins can be forgiven. "If you forgive the sins of any, they are forgiven" (Jn. 20, 23).

What must be revealed to the world, and to Christians, is that there exists a remission of sins. This means that there is no such thing as a definitive failure; there is no evil that cannot be remedied. It means that God proposes to us a plan of redemption which excels any plan that might have been, had we not sinned: "O God, you wondrously ennobled human nature in creating it, and even more wondrously restored it." God would not have permitted evil if he were not able to draw good from it.

The history of the world is a dialogue between God and man. God leaves a man free to go against his designs and to introduce evil and suffering into the world. But every human initiative is matched by divine response. God unceasingly proposes to us splendid reparations of our ravages. Everything will be more beautiful than if we had not sinned. God can transform each of our faults into a happy fault.

We will not enter heaven until all of our faults have been made into happy faults. Then we will be so emptied of ourselves and so filled with God that we will no longer feel any resentment or shame for having sinned. We will enter heaven poor, stripped of our pride, and marveling over the goodness of God.

Let us now try to discern the reasons why we have lost the joy of forgiveness.

First of all, we must distinguish between two very different religions. There is on the one hand the religion of what we do for God—sacrifices, mortifications, penances, all of those difficult and unpleasant things we do for God. This is the religion of people who begrudge doing a favor for God; they act as though they are God's benefactors. They say to themselves, "Look at all that I do for him." They also say to themselves, "What has he ever done for me?"

Our Lord has spoken of these people in his parable of the workers in the vineyard. They are jealous of those who will be accepted into heaven with not having made even half the effort which they themselves have made. They are indignant at the Lord's generosity to others. To their way of thinking, heaven has a price which not God but man must pay.

The other religion is that of what God does for us—the great things he does for us in our misery, the wonderful acts of kindness and mercy by which he fashioned our salvation. In this religion, no one ever tires of rejoicing in praise and thanksgiving to the Lord. This is the religion of the Magnificat, of the Gloria, of the Credo, of the Benedictus, of the Eucharist. "It is truly right and just, proper and helpful towards salvation, that we always and everywhere give thanks to you, O Lord."

In the first religion, to confess is to examine one's conscience, to withdraw into one's self, to draw up an inventory of one's sins. Then one enters into a dark chamber and says to someone unknown—or to someone too well known—things one would prefer not to say. Then one does his penance.

Judas confessed this way. He reflected on his conduct and was filled with remorse. He prepared his confession and entered the confessional of the temple, looking for the priests, though he found only merciless Pharisees; and to them he made his confession: "I have sinned in betraying innocent blood" (Mt. 27, 4). He then did his penance, which was to give back the thirty pieces of silver. But as we know, Judas had no confidence in divine mercy. He had no joyful trust that his sin would be forgiven him. In his despair he went out and hanged himself.

We ought to compare this confession to that of Peter, who made neither an examination of conscience nor an admission of sin. But he saw Christ. He saw Jesus, humiliated and insulted, going across the court of Caiaphas. Jesus looked at him forgivingly, and Peter at once repented. He cried for a long while, in sorrow for having sinned, but even more out of wonder for having been so loved by his Lord.

The conclusion is not that we should not confess our sins. It is that the aim of penance is not above all a moral but a religious one. Penance is an encounter with the Lord in which we learn that he is living, that he loves us and will forgive us. Confession is not so much a cleansing of one's self so that one's conscience can be clear, as it is a means of sacramentally associating ourselves more closely with God. We renounce sin not in order to feel better, but because sin separates us from God.

Thus it is a joy to see our faults—for to recognize our true sins is proof that God is at work within us, leading us to holiness. It is a sign that he is helping us to go beyond our sins, for to see our sins is to have worked loose from them, to move a little bit away from them.

We cannot know God without recognizing ourselves as

sinners. But to see ourselves as sinners is to begin to know God.

God reveals our faults to us with an infinite tenderness. As with Thomas, he does not want to humiliate or reproach us; he only wants us to see what we are.

We ought to cry out with joy and gratitude and confidence that God is speaking to us, that he is declaring himself to us, that he is acting within us. We are not faithful, but he is faithful. We are not persevering, but he is persevering. He will complete in us all that he has begun.

We ought to thank God for giving us the grace to recognize our "countless sins, offenses, and negligences," our lack of faith and love and confidence; but we ought to thank God for making this realization bearable, because we know that God is kind and loving even though we are unworthy.

God forgives, and God alone forgives. He forgives so well, so joyfully, that we are not humiliated by our sins but joyful that they are forgiven. We forget our sins and think only of God's love for us. This is the joy of penance.

Thomas knew this great joy. He never felt happier or more loved than when he was taken into the cloak of Christ.

Peter also knew this joy. His penance was to become the first pope. "You will be a good confessor," the Lord no doubt said to him. "You will know how to forgive sins, now that I have taught you. You will know how to turn the faults of others, like your own, into happy faults."

Peter and Thomas learned personally from the Lord how

to fulfill the precept of the Lord's Prayer: "Forgive us our trespasses, as we forgive those who trespass against us." They were sent out to proclaim the forgiveness of sins; they forgave others, just as they themselves had been forgiven.

Like those two apostles, we must not only come to be forgiven, but must also forgive others. Not to forgive others means that we have not opened ourselves to the Lord. It is a sign, too, that we have not forgiven ourselves—and this is one thing that God cannot forgive us. Hell is the place where people go when they have refused forgiveness. There would be no hell if man imitated the mercy of God.

The priest is thus the representative of the community; he is the witness of the Church. He forgives the sinner in the name of their brothers. It is unfortunate that this communal sacrament has been isolated in the solitary confessional, for in the absolution there is no visible reincorporation of the penitent into the community. Let us pray that the communal dimension of this sacrament will soon be restored.

The forgiveness, the love, and the joy of our brothers ought to be the sacrament, the sensible sign, of the forgiveness, the love, and the joy of God.

THE FIFTH STATION

PAUL

PAUL was the opposite of Thomas, who thought he did not believe. Saul was much worse—he thought he did believe.

Sure of himself, proud of his traditional religion, Saul of Tarsus detested all innovation. He had been raised in the purest Hebrew customs, and he had studied at Jerusalem with the most famous theologian of the time, Gamaliel. A member of the Pharisee sect, scrupulously faithful to all of the prescriptions of the law, Saul was convinced from the very beginning that he had the true faith in the true God. Thus when the Son of God appeared in the world, Saul was profoundly scandalized.

Saul had his ideas about God, and the person of Jesus Christ did not fit in with them. A man who toils with common laborers, who suffers and dies the death of a common criminal, and who says he is God—that man is an absurd impostor. Jesus was unorthodox, and Saul's religion was an orthodox religion.

Thus, roused to indignation by this heretic, Saul began to persecute the Lord's disciples. He witnessed and approved the murder of Stephen, the first Christian martyr. From house to house he went, seeking Christians, arresting men, women, and children.

Saul had so well defined God that he no longer took the trouble to listen to him. But he was also a fanatic, "breathing threats and murder" (Acts 9, 1). And the only way to change the mind of a fanatic is to knock him out of his tracks. The Lord converted Thomas by taking him into his arms; with Saul he had to use lightning.

In a flash, Saul was knocked down, blinded, dazzled, converted. His catechism was a single sentence: "I am Jesus, whom you are persecuting." He learned that Jesus was God, and that this absurd heretic had suffered and died for him. He heard the good news that God was present.

He was called by his name—Saul. God knew him. God wanted him. Saul learned that God was not a doctrine which one studied and imposed, not some inaccessible supreme being, but someone who was on earth, someone who was vulnerable—who could be persecuted.

It was by a Roman, a member of that legalistic and doctrinaire race, that the best definition of Christianity was given. Festus, summarizing to the king Agrippa the trial of Paul by the Pharisees, spoke of the discussions which the Pharisees had "about one Jesus, who was dead, but whom Paul asserted was alive" (Acts 25, 19).

For too many of us, Jesus is dead. He is risen, of course, but "up there," in heaven. It would be too absurd to think that he was anywhere else.

But for Paul, he was someone living, someone whom he had encountered, someone who still suffered and had need of him.

When will we be seized with that shock of surprise and dread—when we have encountered Jesus living on the altar and in our lives? How long will it be before we cease our persecution of our brothers? How long will we waste the blood of the crucified Lord?

God is pure goodness, pure gift. He is always near, and patiently waits for us to come to him. He is patient in sorrow, in agony, until the end of the world, always revealing himself to us.

How many of us have not yet seen God? How many of us have not yet loved God? How many of us persist in refusing God's gift of himself? How many of us persecute his disciples? The true name of this hostile defiance is blasphemy.

We must fall down on our knees, and, blind to our own preconceived ideas about God, recognize the Jesus whom we persecute. We must learn our catechism: that Jesus loves us, even though we have not yet shown our love for him; that he seeks us out, that he wants us to come to him, that he suffered and died for us.

To love a person is to give him power over us. God loves us, and he has given us that terrible power over him. We can make him suffer terribly. We can scorn him and ignore him.

But the power of love can also be a source of great joy. Only a word spoken to the loved one is sufficient to make him happy. To express our love for him, to try to please him, is to exercise a wonderful power which brings the beloved great joy and happiness.

Paul's vision was of the terrible power he had over the Lord. It was the Lord who suffered the most from Paul's relentless persecutions. Now Christ surrendered himself to Paul; he gave himself over, defenseless. From that moment on, Paul understood what his vocation was; he knew that his life was going to change drastically; he knew that the power he had over God, which he had previously used in order to persecute him, he was now going to use in order to honor him, and serve him, and rejoice with him.

The revelation which must come to us is this: that insignificant and common as we are, God takes great interest in us. God loves us, and therefore depends on us. His joy is diminished if we do not love him.

* * *

Two things were revealed to Paul. The first was the identity of God—"I am Jesus. . . ." The second was what he was doing to God— ". . . whom you are persecuting." Paul learned that he not only had not known the Lord, but that he had resisted him—that he had resisted knowing him. Paul's whole previous apostolate, he found out, had been one of revolt. He had thought he believed in God, but he had only believed in himself.

But Paul also realized, like Thomas, that his fanatic resistance was only the sign of his immense will to believe, an effort to silence a deafening inner voice. It was not God whom Saul had been defending in his persecution of the Christians; it was himself—he had been trying to defend himself against God. But on the road to Damascus he gave up this pretension; he began to listen to the voice within himself.

Revolt and defiance harden a man. This resistance to God is at work in each of us; any excuse will do if it keeps us from meeting God face to face. We know very well that God is just beyond the corner, if we will only go there; that he is on the road to Damascus, if we will only journey there. But we fabricate obstacles upon the path; we look for distractions —not only those of pleasure, but those things which also diverted Saul: hard work, "virtue," frantic activity, fidelity to the letter.

Yet one day, like Paul, we must accept to listen to the word of God; we must recognize the Lord, even though we have tried our best to ignore him. Though we think we see, we must be blinded by the light.

The Lord told Saul, "Rise and enter the city, and you will be told what you are to do" (Acts 9, 6). The Lord sends him, as he does all of us, towards the others.

He who would one day be St. Paul, who was to evangelize the nations, whom the Lord honored with a vision, whom the Lord personally and spectacularly converted—he was ordered to go to Damascus and beg instructions from a simple disciple named Ananias, whose only superiority over Paul was that he belonged to the Christian Church. The hand of the Lord made Paul blind, but it was from the hands of a believer that he was to recover his sight.

"They led him by the hand and brought him into Damascus. And for three days he was without sight, . . ." (Acts 9, 8–9). The first thing which the Lord asked of him was that he let himself be led—to renounce initiative, to accept to see no longer in the old way, to make a retreat for three days.

And Paul, hot-tempered and impetuous, meekly accepted. He did the only thing there was to do, the only thing the Lord expected from him at that time: he prayed. "Now the Lord said to Ananias in a vision, 'Rise and go to the street called Straight, and inquire in the house of Judas for a man of Tarsus named Saul; for behold, he is praying'" (Acts 9, 11).

Ananias had not much enthusiasm for preaching this retreat, however. He tried to dissuade the Lord: "I have heard from many about this man, how much evil he has done to thy saints at Jerusalem" (Acts 9, 13). Ananias was cautious, well informed, apprehensive. "But the Lord said to him, 'Go, for he is a chosen instrument of mine to carry my name before the Gentiles and kings and the sons of Israel; for I will show him how much he must suffer for the sake of my name'" (Acts 9, 15–16).

So Ananias went to seek out Paul—even though the Lord did not want to listen to reason; and once in the house on Straight street he laid his hands upon him, saying, "Brother Saul, the Lord Jesus who appeared to you on the road . . .

has sent me that you may regain your sight and be filled with the Holy Spirit" (Acts 9, 18). And Paul immediately recovered his sight.

This is a parable about the Church—that even the weakest priests can nevertheless dispense grace, that they can authentically communicate the sacramental life.

Our practical way of believing in Christ will be to believe in his Church, to believe in one another; we will have to be like Ananias, and believe the Lord even though he seems to be wrong; and we will have to believe in those people like Ananias—regardless of what they appear to be—who are called by God to dispense his life-giving grace.

We do not have true faith if God always acts the way we want him to. As long as our desires coincide with the desires of God, we have not yet made the act of faith. To have faith is to accept to go in the direction opposite of the one we want to take; it is to recognize the presence of the Lord in people whom we dislike; it is to believe in the Church even though there are things about the Church which scandalize us. The road of faith is unchartable, arduous, and very long.

Faith is thus a living and ever new reality—like the God to whom it is addressed. It is the act of confidence we make to God each day and at each moment of the day, by trying to see him in every event, in every person, in every feeling within our heart. To have faith is to regard as unimportant what is most important to us. It is to listen to what we do not desire to hear. It is to love those whom we do not wish to love.

Faith does not give us a choice, other than wholly to commit ourselves to do the will of God; faith is a life spent in discovering God. Faith makes us true contemplatives.

The road of faith is arduous and very long. But there is a Friend who will meet us there and guide us on our way. The road of faith is thus a way of joy.

THE SIXTH STATION

MARY

We could not very well speak of joy without speaking of the Blessed Virgin, to whom we pray that she will help transform our present sorrows into lasting joy.

Mary had one apparition in her life, one only—the annunciation—but it was enough for her forever. It dispensed her forever from other apparitions. The final beatitude was true of her even then: "Blessed are those who have not seen and yet believe."

To have faith, it has been said, is to remain faithful in darkness to what has been seen in light. Mary listened so well to the word of the angel that she kept it all her life, she was nourished by it all her life, she always believed, with her whole soul, "that he would save his people," that "of his kingdom there would be no end," that "with God nothing is impossible."

Mary was the only one who did not despair when Jesus died; she was the only one who was not separated from him, even though he had been put away in the tomb.

At the time of the annunciation, she alone in the name of the Church received Christ in faith; and at the time of his death, she alone in the name of the Church received him in faith. She was the sole burning lamp in the sanctuary; her faith was not extinguished.

During the time of the passion and death of Jesus, Mary suffered as much as one can humanly suffer; but her faith in her Lord never wavered, nor did her hope, nor her total confidence in the Father, in the mysterious necessity and efficacy of all that was happening.

After the death of Jesus on Calvary, Mary shrouded the outraged body of her son with the same piety, tenderness, and infinite respect with which she formerly, as a young mother, had cared for the fragile body entrusted to her. Nothing of the despair of Mary Magdalene came into her heart, for though Jesus had stopped being alive in his own body, he could never die in the heart of his mother.

When Jesus descended into sheol, to rest before ascending to his Father, he was also in communion with his mother.

Jesus rose from the tomb on the third day, not to console his mother—for she was radiant with joy—but to dispatch the others to where Mary was waiting for them. And when they ran up to Mary to tell her the good news that her son was alive, they saw that she already knew. From that moment on, they began to understand her place in the Church. Gradually they began to seek her out, to sit by her side and feel at ease with her, for they knew that she understood them. During the ten days following Pentecost and before the ascension, they stayed with her always; she was a refuge, a source of faith. She was protecting the new-found Church.

Mary, mother of the apostles, never preached, nor did she go out into the apostolate. But she communicated the true presence of God. For thirty years she had never gone out from her home, for she knew that within it was the salvation of the world. And then one day the whole Church came to her. As she had lovingly taken care of her son our Lord, so now she lovingly watched over his small band of disciples who were to go out and change the world.

Each of us has the same incredible vocation which Mary had—to give life to God in the world, to make God alive in the world.

The angel of the annunciation still hovers over the world, seeking a servant of the Lord—someone simple enough, trusting enough, to admit without understanding that in himself also the word will become flesh and dwell among men.

THE ASCENSION

In order to celebrate the ascension of our Lord, it is first of all necessary to understand the radical difference between a disappearance and a departure. A departure causes an absence; a disappearance inaugurates a hidden presence.

Our Lord did not depart from us when he ascended into heaven; he did not leave us behind, deserting us and leaving us as orphans. He remains with us forever, until the end of the world. By ascending into heaven, he became fully glorified, exalted, spiritualized in his humanity—and thus became more intimately related to us than ever before.

Jesus sits at the right hand of the Father. But where is the Father? St. John tells us that he is with us, in us, on this earth, forever: "If a man loves me, he will keep my word, and my Father will love him, and we will come to him and make our home with him" (Jn. 14, 23). A home is much more than a presence. We can go to many places, but we dwell only at home—and our Lord and his Father want to make their home in us!

When we pray to "Our Father, who art in heaven," we are not signifying that he is in some remote place; we are simply asserting his omnipotence. Christ shares in this omnipotence by his ascension—"He ascended far above all the heavens, that he might fill all things" (Eph. 4, 10): the preface for the feast of the ascension adds, "so that he might make us sharers in his own divinity."

The Lord's ascension was an ascension in power, in efficacy, and therefore it was an intensification of his presence. Just as Christ did not leave his Father when he became incarnate as man, so he did not depart from us when he ascended to his Father. On the contrary, he established more direct communication between man and God.

Christ remains the most active and the most present person in the world. That is what St. Mark says in such a striking way in his narrative on the ascension. "The Lord Jesus . . . was taken up into heaven, and sat down at the right hand of God" (Mk. 16, 19). But Mark continues, "The apostles went forth and preached everywhere, while the Lord worked with them and confirmed the message by the signs that attended it" (Mk. 16, 20).

What a great joy this is: that the Lord is here, on earth, with us, and that he will never leave us; his spiritualized presence has reached an intensity and an extension which his bodily presence could not attain.

It was to our advantage that the Lord ascended into heaven. In this way we can find him present everywhere—in prayer and in action, in the sacraments, in our brothers, in any place where his grace is at work, which is everywhere.